THE BIRTHDAY RULES:
CRITICAL CONVERSATIONS TO HAVE
WITH YOUR CHILDREN

THE BIRTHDAY RULES:
CRITICAL CONVERSATIONS TO HAVE WITH YOUR CHILDREN
(AGES 6 TO 16)

JEFF WALD WITH DR. RACHEL MARSH

A POST HILL PRESS BOOK

The Birthday Rules:
Critical Conversations to Have with Your Children
© 2017 by Jeff Wald with Dr. Rachel Marsh
All Rights Reserved

ISBN: 978-1-68261-244-6
ISBN (eBook): 978-1-68261-245-3

Cover Design by Quincy Alivio
Interior Design and Composition by Greg Johnson/Textbook Perfect

Post Hill Press
posthillpress.com

Printed in Canada
Published in the United States of America

Contents

The Birthday Rules: An Introduction

In a fast-paced world consisting of ever-changing technology and evolving social norms, parents are finding the traditional challenges of raising well-adjusted, self-confident and socially responsible children ever more difficult. Parents struggle with when to grant certain permissions and when to have difficult conversations. They tend to avoid such decisions, waiting until an external event forces the conversation or too many kids at school have been granted the same permission. To meet these challenges, parents need a framework that can adjust to the development needs of each child, the values of each community and the means of each family. What we offer in these pages is a suggested framework that we call *The Birthday Rules*.

The Birthday Rules provides a fun and flexible framework of an "annual review" process combined with a structure for increasing permissions, responsibilities and conversations. We suggest using a child's birthday as not only a time to celebrate and have cake, but also as an excellent opportunity to have important conversations, grant desired permissions and explain the responsibilities that go along with those permissions.

While there can never be the perfect guide to raising children, we can create a structure to help with some of the most important tasks parents have: creating a safe environment to communicate and demonstrate unconditional love.

The Birthday Rules offers a guide as to the appropriate ages for certain activities and conversations:

- When should children be allowed to have mobile devices?
- When should discussions of bullying take place?
- When will children be responsible enough to surf the Internet on their own?
- When should a discussion of sexual activity take place? What about safe sex?
- When should discussions about depression and suicide take place?

Parents have debated some of these questions for centuries; others are new concerns in our modern, technology-enabled world. Either way, parents have the opportunity to have conversations with their children, from toddlers to teenagers, to better prepare them for the inevitable situations they will face as they develop.

The annual conversation that occurs around a child's birthday is formatted to create a safe and effective environment for parents to discuss difficult topics, create appropriate permissions, and then align the responsibilities that go with those permissions.

We do not profess to be experts on child development, but instead have taken the necessary time reading material and studies from many experts and compiling the data into this quick workbook for you and your child.

How It Works

The Birthday Rules is about proactive parenting. *The Birthday Rules* is about creating a safe and consistent communication channel. *The Birthday Rules* is about open and honest dialogue. *The Birthday Rules* is about unconditional love.

Each chapter of *The Birthday Rules* features a list of recommended guidelines and discussion topics for children ages six to sixteen. Topics are revisited as the perspective or focus of the conversation changes over time. *The Birthday Rules* are designed for modification, which is why each chapter will contain space for "Your Rules and Conversations."

When a new permission is suggested, parents must be clear about the responsibilities that permission entails and the consequences of failing to meet those responsibilities. The conversation topics should be started when a child is capable of handling the discussion. This is a forum for very open discussion and very candid answers. An unfiltered and unguided view on all these topics is a click away for your child; this is your chance to frame the discussion in a healthy and proactive way.

How the Rules are enforced becomes a critical part of the framework. Each chapter has a place to review the previous year (or years) Rules and Conversations, called the "Progress Report." If a child has not followed the Rules for specific permission, you may consider delaying future permissions (certainly other milestone dates beyond the birthday can be used). How you enforce the Rules is a choice each parent must make, and in many ways enforcement is the most difficult part of parenting. *The Birthday Rules* framework is an aid to structure a consistent response.

In addition, a "What's Going On" section is included for each year, outlining the new discoveries and challenges children and parents typically face at these ages.

Certain events may trigger a conversation prior to when the collective research has indicated a child may be ready. You should always engage in those conversations when a child needs to talk about them. *The Birthday Rules* is not designed to replace any conversations, but rather to augment and help when conversations are difficult to have.

Again, every parent and child is different, so families should feel free to adopt *The Birthday Rules* as it best fits their values, parenting style, and child's unique development.

Introducing Your Children to *The Birthday Rules*

Before the first meeting, explain to your child what this process is all about, why it's important, and how it will work. Some key points to make:

- You are old enough for us to talk about your future and when you are going to be able to do and learn about certain things.
- On each birthday from now until you are sixteen, we can sit down and discuss the previous year and your progress.
- Each year we will discuss new permissions, things you can do, and items you can have.
- Each of those new permissions comes with serious responsibilities, and we will talk about what you need to do to maintain these permissions.
- We will also talk about topics that are important to your growth, health and well-being.
- You can look at this book anytime, and we will keep notes on the things we want to accomplish together.

Ready to get started?

The Recommended Rules and Conversations for Six-Year-Olds

AGE
6

What should children be learning about at age 6?

YOUR RULES AND CONVERSATION TOPICS

What else do you want to talk about?

_____

_____

_____

_____

_____

_____

_____

_____

_____

_____

1. Eye Contact
2. Manners
3. Privacy Rules
4. Feelings
5. Table Manners
6. Allowance Rules
7. Take Care of Your Body

Parent's Guide to Age 6

What's Going On?

By age six, most kids are enrolled in kindergarten or have just completed it. They have a good grip on gross motor skills such as jumping, throwing a ball, and running. At the same time, they are still developing fine motor skills that require the coordination of small muscle movements, such as using scissors to cut paper or a knife to cut food.

Aside from obvious physical developments, you can expect to see changes in your child's:

- Social behavior (learning to navigate friendships).

- Intellectual development (learning through language, comprehending abstract thinking).

- Emotional expression (getting feelings hurt more easily and becoming more aware of other people's feelings).

These changes, in particular, warrant several critical conversations with your six-year-old—who needs your help navigating the transition from "little kid" to "big kid."

Suggested Rules and Conversations

1. **Eye Contact.** *Eye contact shows that you are paying attention and care about what the person who is talking is saying.* Eye contact is a core social skill that helps children learn to give others their full attention. While your kids will pick up on the importance of eye contact by your example, experts recommend asking children, "Please look into my eyes." Explain that making eye contact means you are interested in other people and what they are saying. Remind them to look into other people's eyes while both talking and listening instead of looking at the ground or letting their eyes wander when someone else speaks.

2. **Manners.** *Say "please" and "thank you."* Talk with your kids about the importance of showing gratitude and the appropriate times to say "thank you." Saying "please" is equally critical if you want others to consider your children polite. Model this behavior for them, and remind them to use it when they ask for anything. In addition, manners at this age include teaching children to use their "inside voices."

   Remember that children who understand social nuances and express social graces are noticed by others. Consider role-playing with your kids when you're expecting guests or before they meet someone new. Practice greeting the other person, shaking hands, introducing themselves, saying "Nice to meet you" and "good-bye."

3. **Privacy Rules.** *Knock before entering a room with a closed door.* Depending on the boundaries you set in your home, this could mean teaching your children not to open a closed door without knocking, eavesdrop on private conversations, or read private things not meant for their eyes.

   Respect private communications. Children at this age need to understand that not all conversations are meant for everyone. They need to have boundaries and rules in place to learn how to discern when a conversation is not for them.

   Respect emails (and other private messages), and don't read them. Just as children need to learn boundaries with verbal conversations, they also need to understand the basic societal rules about respecting privacy on email and other messaging tools.

4. **Feelings.** *Name your feelings, and respect other people's feelings.* At age six children begin to understand their own feelings and recognize the feelings of others. The discussions at this point should center on expressing empathy in a respectful manner and learning to say "I'm sorry" when they hurt someone's

feelings. One caution: Experts warn that forced apologies can teach young children to be insincere. However, it's important to explain the power of an apology to repair hurt feelings and relationships.

5. **Table Manners.** *We have special manners that are necessary when eating.* Talk to your children about sitting at the table when eating, usage of utensils, including when to use a fork, knife, or spoon and how to use them quietly, keeping their mouths closed while chewing, taking small bites instead of big ones, and offering the last portion of something to others first. Also teach them to keep toys and gadgets away from the table so they can focus on conversation with family and friends.

6. **Allowance Rules.** *With money comes responsibility.* Before you talk to your child, consider your own philosophy on giving allowances. There's no right or wrong way to handle giving an allowance, but before having the conversation, parents first need to decide the rules around an allowance.

Rules include when to start giving an allowance, what amount the children will receive and how often, and what tasks or behaviors should be required for getting it. An allowance can be a reward for household tasks—cleaning their rooms, washing dishes, taking out the trash—or for doing something extra, beyond their stated chores.

Regardless of your rules, any discussion about allowance is an opportunity to teach children how money works. Children should come away from the conversation understanding that with money comes responsibility.

7. **Take Care of Your Body.** *Always feel free to ask questions about anything that has to do with your body and your health.* Start this conversation about the importance of taking care of themselves, and differentiating the things that are harmful or good for their bodies.

The Recommended Rules and Conversations for Seven-Year-Olds

What should children be learning about at age 7?

YOUR RULES AND CONVERSATION TOPICS
What else do you want to talk about?

_____

_____

_____

_____

PROGRESS REPORT
What's happened since last year?

_____

_____

_____

_____

1. More Responsibility Around the House
2. Help Other People
3. Patience
4. Safety
5. Do Not Put Yourself or Others Down
6. Set a Good Example
7. Unsupervised Video Games and TV Rules
8. Swear Words

Parent's Guide to Age 7

What's Going On?

Seven-year-olds are going through a major life transition. No longer small children, they are able to think, feel, and empathize in new ways. They thrive on new challenges, adventures, and goals—though they often need encouragement to try these new things. During this age, parents can instill confidence and self-worth and help their child learn foundational skills for success in life.

Suggested Rules and Conversations

1. **More Responsibility Around the House.** *Learn to help around the house and take on more responsibilities.* By age seven, children are capable of taking on more responsibility. This usually starts with an allowance, but small chores and assigned tasks around the house empower them to see their value and learn about hard work. They also learn about consequences when they fail to follow through. Making your children take responsibility for simple tasks now can help teach life-long skills and values that will serve them well in school, life, and work.

2. **Help Other People.** *Practice compassion for those less fortunate than you.* At this age, children begin to understand empathy and sympathy for others. Teach your children compassion by initiating conversations about why it is important to give both time and resources to people in need. Talk to them about ways to help. Consider volunteering together as a family.

3. **Patience.** *Practice being patient, even when you don't get your way.* Many young children are used to getting things their own way, on their own timelines. However, parents know this is not how life works in the adult world. By age seven, children should understand what patience means. Help your children practice patience by pointing out opportunities

where they need to use it, noting when they are being impatient.

4. **Safety.** *Always notice your surroundings and be mindful of your safety.* Parents can start instilling an awareness of surroundings into their child around age seven. At this age, they can comprehend ways to be safe in different surroundings and how to be observant.

5. **Do Not Put Yourself or Others Down.** *It's never good to judge or talk down to others, remember that every person is unique.* At this age, many children strive for perfection. This is also when they start to feel peer pressure and are more observant of how other people see them. Instill self-esteem in your child by accepting and developing the unique individuals that they are. At this point, their self-esteem can be very fragile, so be sure to offer frequent encouragement and positive feedback. Parents also need to talk to their child about the self-esteem of friends and it can be negative to put others down.

6. **Set a Good Example.** *Younger kids look up to you so make sure you are patient and kind.* Seven-year-old children are very capable and can pass on what they've learned to younger siblings, relatives, or friends. By encouraging your child to be a mentor and to set a good example for younger children, you reinforce both good behavior and self-esteem in your seven-year-old. Praising them for being positive leaders among peers at this age can help prevent them from being swayed by negative peer pressure as they grow older.

7. **Unsupervised Video Games and TV Rules.** *Video games and other electronics are a privilege, not an entitlement.* Limit video game and TV time to set hours, after children have completed their homework and chores. By age seven, most children have already begun to play video games of some sort—at home, at school, and while at friends' homes. This can be a positive activity, both for motor skills development as

well as social bonding with peers. However, not all video games are appropriate for children, nor is playing them around the clock. Talk to your children about the rules and expectations that go along with the privilege of playing video games— including which games or parental ratings you approve of, how many hours they're allowed to play, rules about sharing with siblings, and any other pertinent guidelines.

Most seven-year-olds are capable of making intelligent decisions about television shows. In fact, children ages seven and older spend the vast majority of their television time unsupervised. As with video games, set clear rules about the amount of time and types of programming you find acceptable for children, and outline the consequences for disobeying these rules.

8. **Swear Words.** *Just because you may hear adults say certain words doesn't mean you can say them.* By around age six or seven, children start picking up on "bad words" in the conversations around them. They will mimic and learn that they can attract attention by using these inappropriate words. Talk to your children about what swearing is, and where it is or is not acceptable given your family values and rules. Remember, they are going to hear these words anyway, so this is your time to frame them appropriately.

The Recommended Rules and Conversations for Eight-Year-Olds

AGE

8

What should children be learning about at age 8?

YOUR RULES AND CONVERSATION TOPICS
What else do you want to talk about?

_____

_____

_____

_____

PROGRESS REPORT
What's happened since last year?

_____

_____

_____

_____

1. Opinions
2. Homework Rules
3. Friendship
4. Personal Hygiene Rules
5. Devices Rules
6. Unsupervised Internet Access Rules
7. Community Service
8. Supervised Account Rules

Parent's Guide to Age 8

What's Going On?

Eight-year-old children are starting to form opinions about themselves and the world. They are slowly embracing independence and can take responsibility for many tasks, including chores, homework, and personal hygiene. They are developing friendships and learning how to interact respectfully with their peers. During this shift, parents can empower eight-year-olds to become even more independent—both in thoughts and actions.

Suggested Rules and Conversations

1. **Opinions.** *Learn to share opinions and viewpoints in a way that is both productive and respectful to people who might disagree.* Eight-year-olds often have strong opinions, and this is the age where many begin sharing their viewpoints on a variety of topics. Encourage your children to develop and question their opinions and to understand why they have certain viewpoints. Talk to them about how to share their ideas in appropriate and respectful ways, especially in the presence of adults or other children who might think differently.

2. **Homework Rules.** *Complete homework and chores without being asked.* While children at this age can handle many tasks on their own, they often lack the discipline to do so. Talk to your children about the importance of self-discipline and completing simple tasks without being reminded. Help them learn skills to manage homework schedules, morning routines, and other responsibilities. Explain that this is not a punishment but rather an important part of growing up. This helps children get excited about being independent, instead of feeling overwhelmed by their new responsibilities.

3. **Friendship.** *Choose your friends wisely—they are a reflection of you.* By this age, children are learning they can choose their friends. Earlier in life, they probably played with whoever was nearby, at an arranged playdate or group setting. As children begin forming opinions about personalities and the types of people they enjoy spending time with, it's important to instill a healthy approach to friendships. Encourage your children to form friendships with others who can have a positive influence on them.

  Explain that while they get to choose their friends, they shouldn't leave others out or ignore new people. Discuss both the enjoyable and difficult aspects of friendships and what it means to be a good friend.

4. **Personal Hygiene Rules.** *Take regular showers, brush your teeth at least twice a day, and take pride in your appearance.* Reinforce good personal hygiene habits. While eight-year-olds are capable of keeping themselves clean, they might need reminders. This is your opportunity to make healthy hygiene a normal thought process for your child.

5. **Devices Rules.** *Take good care of computers and other expensive electronic devices.* Eight-year-olds need to learn basic respect of technological devices, as they are at an age where they start to use these unsupervised. Parents can teach their child basic rules of how to use and take care of computers and other pieces of technology.

6. **Unsupervised Internet Access Rules.** *When you are online, only access websites, apps, and content that have been approved by parents or teachers.* By age eight, most children can be trusted to use digital devices unsupervised. They know how to operate and respect the equipment and software programs, and in our digital age, children rely on computers and the Internet for learning. In fact, by age eight, a vast majority of parents permit their children

to use online devices and services. Before granting your children unsupervised Internet access, talk to them about your rules and expectations for them online—including which websites and types of content you feel are appropriate at their age. Children need to understand their limits and know they will be held accountable for their Internet usage.

7. **Community Service.** *Helping people in the community is a privilege and should be practiced throughout your life.* Even at the age of eight, children can understand empathy and comprehend when someone needs help. While they are still too young to do some projects, there are plenty of ways that children can help serve their community. Talk to your child about ways they can help so that they can learn to have a viewpoint of community service as they grow and develop.

8. **Supervised Account Rules.** *Do not use online accounts without a parent's or teacher's permission and supervision.* Federal laws prohibit online companies—including email providers—from collecting information from children under thirteen years of age. However, starting around age eight, many children create accounts under fake names and birthdays. Some parents create accounts for their children so they can play games or access educational content online. If your underage children are asking for accounts—or already have access—talk to them about how to use their accounts appropriately, including the dangers of responding to messages from strangers. It is also a good idea to monitor their use, at least in the beginning, to ensure they understand and adhere to your rules.

The Recommended Rules and Conversations for Nine-Year-Olds

What should children be learning about at age 9?

YOUR RULES AND CONVERSATION TOPICS
What else do you want to talk about?

_____

_____

_____

_____

PROGRESS REPORT
What's happened since last year?

_____

_____

_____

_____

1. Sex
2. Influence of Media
3. Peer Pressure
4. Consequences
5. Extracurricular Activities Rules
6. Goals
7. Judgment

Parent's Guide to Age 9

What's Going On?

Nine-year-old children are soaking in lots of information from television, the media, and their friends. To help them form healthy opinions about themselves and the world, they also need to hear positive messages from their parents. Children at this age are also participating in new extracurricular and school settings, and they need guidance to handle these new experiences.

Suggested Rules and Conversations

1. **Sex.** *Come to parents, not friends or the Internet, with any questions about sex.* Age nine might seem too early to talk to your children about sex, but many preteens are already experimenting with sexual acts. So, it's important to educate your children before they hear about sex from other kids, the Internet, or television. Open the dialogue, and ensure your children know they can (and should) come to you with questions.

2. **Influence of Media.** *Recognize and resist the influence of media on your thoughts and behavior.* Children at this age are very aware of what is happening in the media. They might feel pressured to act or look like people they see on TV or try to change their personalities to fit what they see modeled by famous people. This is your opportunity to teach your children about the positive and negative messages that media in our culture sends.

3. **Peer Pressure.** *If peers are pressuring you to do something that seems wrong or feels uncomfortable, discuss it with parents or teachers.* We all know how strong peer pressure can be for children, teens, and even adults. Talk to your child about peer pressure, what to expect, how to handle it, and why it's important to make choices for the right reasons, not just to impress others.

4. **Consequences.** *Remember that your actions have consequences.* Nine-year-olds still need structure to understand that there are consequences for their actions. At this age, they are wise enough to look for loopholes and brave enough to test their limits. Set clear rules and outline the consequences of breaking them. Bad behavior needs discipline, and children need rules to learn how to behave in social situations.

5. **Extracurricular Activities Rules.** *Understand that extracurricular activities are a privilege and that schoolwork comes first.* By this age, children have many options for extracurricular activities. Sometimes children are shy and nervous about trying new things. Others might be so excited that they want to jump into too many activities at once. Encourage your children to try new things. Talk to them about which activities they want to do and why, and help them narrow down their options. Refrain from over-scheduling your children.

6. **Goals.** *Set goals for yourself, and stick to them.* Bolster your children's self-esteem by helping them realize just how much they're capable of accomplishing. Offer encouragement and support for taking on new challenges, and help them set achievable personal goals. This teaches them to derive confidence from personal achievement rather than rely on others for their sense of self-worth.

7. **Judgment.** *Put yourself in other people's shoes before you judge them, and try to understand where they're coming from.* Most nine-year-old children are capable of comprehending other people's emotions and considering the feelings of others, but they might need encouragement to think this way. Foster empathy in your children by talking to them about how others might feel in different situations. Encourage them to put themselves in others' shoes by asking, "How do you think that made them feel?"

The Recommended Rules and Conversations for Ten-Year-Olds

What should children be learning about at age 10?

YOUR RULES AND CONVERSATION TOPICS
What else do you want to talk about?

_____

_____

_____

_____

PROGRESS REPORT
What's happened since last year?

_____

_____

_____

_____

Parent's Guide to Age 10

What's Going On?

By age ten, children have become fairly independent and are capable of deeper thinking than ever before. While they can—and want to—do more alone, they still need plenty of guidance to process life, grow into emotional maturity, and better understand life experiences and relationships.

Suggested Rules and Conversations

1. **Rules.** *Follow all school and household rules without constant reminders.* Ten-year-olds are still very much children, and they still need rules, discipline, and instruction from parents. At this age, it's important to help children understand why the rules are in place—not only for the immediate scenarios but also for the bigger picture. Explaining your reasons— and not just "because I said so"— will help your children make better decisions in the long term and be successful with rules and constraints as they grow older.

   Understand the consequences of breaking rules. By age ten, most children are emotionally mature enough to navigate many problems and relationship challenges, but they still need help from parents to navigate the new emotions that come with age. Encourage your children to talk to you about challenging emotions and relationships and to ask for your advice about conflicts that arise with their peers.

2. **Ask for Help with School Work.** *Never be afraid to ask for help with your schoolwork or time management.* By age ten, children have greater cognitive thinking skills and can process more complex thoughts. School projects and homework become more challenging as teachers begin to expect more from students. Many ten-year-olds struggle to handle the heavier workloads and meet their

teachers' high expectations. Talk to your children about their concerns and how to better manage their time. Encourage them to come to you if they need extra help or resources.

3. **Family Time.** *Along with friends, hobbies, and extracurricular activities, make time for your family.* Ten-year-old children often pull away from family time, and this is perfectly natural. They are developing friendships and relationships away from the home as well as their own interests outside of family activities. Encourage your child to talk about the important friendships and hobbies in their life and to make time for family as well.

4. **Home Alone.** *When home alone, remember that all normal rules apply—and maybe a few extra ones.* By age ten most children are ready to be home alone. Ten-year-olds are often mature enough that parents can trust them to stay home alone for short periods of time. If you feel your children are ready to be unsupervised, make sure that they know where emergency information is located, what to do in a variety of different scenarios, and how to reach you with questions. Remind them that all household rules still apply when you aren't home and that breaking your trust will have consequences.

5. **Supervised Social Media Rules.** *Do not use social media without parental permission.* By age ten, more than half of children are on social media of some kind. In fact, most eight- to thirteen-year-olds ignore Facebook's age restriction and join anyway. Even more alarming, almost half have messaged strangers, starting from an average age of twelve. Talk to your children about the possible dangers of social media, and ensure they know you'll be monitoring their activity. Set rules and limitations, and clearly outline the consequences of social media abuse.

Never message strangers on social media. Parents need to talk to their ten-year-old about the importance of being safe on social media and the potentially harmful situations that can arise from messaging and interacting with strangers online. Children at this age do not think about all of the dangers that can arise from messaging strangers, and therefore need to be reminded of those potential dangers.

Do not say anything on social media you wouldn't say in person. A healthy approach to communication on social media needs to start young given that users of social media often start young. Teach your child what is appropriate to say and do on social media at a young age, so that they form healthy habits to follow as they grow older.

6. **Middle School.** *Talk to parents about any fears, anxieties, or questions regarding middle school.* By age ten, children are preparing to enter middle school. Moving on from elementary school can be either a scary or exciting prospect, depending on each child's personality and school experience thus far. Talk your children through any fears, anxieties, excitement, or other emotions to help prepare them for this big change.

7. **Bullying.** *Be kind and compassionate to all your peers, and never bully others.* Ten-year-olds probably encountered bullying in elementary school, but it definitely increases when they begin to interact with older kids in middle school. Talk to your children about how to recognize a bully, what to do if they are being bullied, and how to be an ally when another child is being bullied. Just as importantly, talk to your children about why bullying is unacceptable, and discuss the consequences they will face if you find out they are engaging in this behavior.

8. **Unsupervised Texting Rules.**
   You may text with your friends unsupervised. With texting there are one-to-one interactions and this is the first place to give you child some online social independence. Other social media platforms have very public posts and may be seen outside a trusted circle, while an initial text is just to its recipients. You should explain how texts (and photos) can be forwarded and the consequences of communication that is always tracked.

The Recommended Rules and Conversations for Eleven-Year-Olds

AGE

11

What should children be learning about at age 11?

YOUR RULES AND CONVERSATION TOPICS
What else do you want to talk about?

_____

_____

_____

_____

PROGRESS REPORT
What's happened since last year?

_____

_____

_____

_____

_____

1. Friendship
2. Sexual Activity
3. Independent Thinking
4. Decision Making
5. Device Time Rules
6. Supervised Mobile Phone Rules
7. Drugs and Alcohol

Parent's Guide to Age 11

What's Going On?

Developmental psychologists generally recognize age eleven as the beginning of formal operational thinking. Eleven-year-old children reason with more adult-like logic and are less dependent on concrete examples. They are investigating independence in thought, personality, and activities—and are now more likely to question authority. Parents need to recognize disrespectful behavior and help their child process their thoughts and emotions in healthy, respectful ways.

Suggested Rules and Conversations

1. **Friendship.** *Treat your friends the way you want them to treat you.* Eleven-year-olds might already have a best friend, but their friendships will start to develop more at this age. They might find themselves drawn to certain friends more than others, and they will start to choose friends based on common interests and personalities, rather than having friends chosen for them by groups or the classes they are in. Talk to your children about how to be a good friend, and explain that people often have different types of friends in life.

2. **Sexual Activity.** *Changes in your bodies are normal—don't be afraid to ask questions about what you are experiencing.* Some children—especially girls—begin to enter puberty around this age, so it's a good time to revisit the "sex talk." Talk to your children about what's happening to their bodies and how they feel about these changes, especially if they're developing faster or slower than their peers. Also discuss what they should do when they have romantic or sexual feelings for their friends and what forms of physical affection are appropriate at this age.

3. **Independent Thinking.** *Learn to express independent thoughts without being disrespectful.* Eleven-year-olds can do many things for themselves and might think of themselves as more grown-up than they really are. While they are starting to have deeper intellectual thoughts, they are still very much children. Encourage your child to try new things and become independent, but make sure they know there are still definitive boundaries at this age and that you are closely monitoring their behavior.

   Around age eleven, children start to understand the bigger picture in life and develop a capacity to reason that they didn't have before. They are more likely to "smart off" and to push boundaries with adults who let them. Talk to your child about the importance of having and demonstrating respect—for parents, teachers, and even their peers.

4. **Decision Making.** *Remember the difference between right and wrong, and make good decisions.* At this age, children start to process the concept of right and wrong and to develop a stronger individual set of values and morals. They question more things and watch the adults around them for cues. Be mindful of your own actions and the example you set for your kids during this time. Talk your children through different experiences and scenarios to help them process and contextualize the concepts of right and wrong.

5. **Device Time Rules.** *Follow all rules and observe set time limits when using devices.* More than likely, your child has been exposed to technology and electronic devices before now. However, children at this age might feel a stronger need to be plugged in and to connect with friends online. Talk to your children about having healthy boundaries when it comes to technology. Discuss limitations and

the consequences for not managing their devices responsibly. Device use has to be balanced with homework, extracurricular activities and family time.

6. **Supervised Mobile Phone Rules.** *Do not get so distracted by your phone and other electronic devices that you ignore the people around you.* By age eleven, most children have phones. This can be a positive thing for both children and their parents. Tweens get to have longer, deeper interactions with friends than they can have at school, and parents can reach children more easily when they're away from home. Before allowing your children to have their own phones; however, talk to them about phone etiquette and other important rules for phone use. Discuss the importance of face-to-face conversations and not ignoring everyone around you while staring at a screen. Set consequences for abusing this privilege, and set a good example for them with your own phone behavior.

Never use your phone at school unless it's an emergency situation and you have permission from your teacher. Parents should talk to their children about the rules of using phones, especially in school settings. Make sure your child is following the rules that a school sets.

Do not give your phone number to strangers or post it online. Many preteens are extremely excited to have a phone. However, they need reminders from their parents about who to give their contact information to and when. They need to understand the implications of sharing their phone number in public places like the Internet.

7. **Drugs and Alcohol.** *You may run into scenarios where drugs or alcohol are around—know that you can ask questions about these things at any time.* Children are getting exposed to drugs and alcohol at earlier ages in our culture because of friends, television, and social media. Your child may be encouraged to try drugs, alcohol, or cigarettes within the next couple of years. Talk to your children about what drugs and alcohol are, and how harmful they are. Open that dialogue early on so that your child feels safe talking to you about this topic and is prepared for what they most likely will be exposed to soon.

AGE

12

1. Stress
2. Feelings
3. Self-Expression
4. Bullying
5. Confidence
6. Smoking
7. Unsupervised Social Media Rules

The Recommended Rules and Conversations for Twelve-Year-Olds

What should children be learning about at age 12?

YOUR RULES AND CONVERSATION TOPICS
What else do you want to talk about?

_____

_____

_____

_____

PROGRESS REPORT
What's happened since last year?

_____

_____

_____

_____

Parent's Guide to Age 12

What's Going On?

Twelve is an age when children are learning to discover who they are. Many are experiencing puberty by this point, but some are not. They are learning to deal with changing emotions, stressors, and personalized opinions. They don't always know how to express what they are feeling and often don't understand that these feelings are normal. Parents need to recognize these changes and encourage their children to process the issues and changes in healthy ways.

Suggested Rules and Conversations

1. **Stress.** *Practice coping skills for stress and anxiety.* Increased demands at school and changing friendships can make this age stressful for many children. Some kids—even those who coped happily enough until now—find social relationships and school life more challenging in these preteen years.

They need to learn new coping skills to help manage stress and anxiety. Explain to your children that stress is a normal part of life, and talk to them about how to deal with these feelings.

2. **Feelings.** *Learn to talk about your feelings without having constant emotional meltdowns.* Along with puberty, children at this age often experience intense emotions they don't know how to process. Moods might seem unpredictable, and these ups and downs can lead to increased conflict, both at school and at home. Teach your children to talk about the complex emotions behind this behavior, and discuss how to handle these feelings without having a meltdown.

   Respect the feelings, opinions, and needs of other people—at school and at home. Pre-teens need to learn to respect the rights, needs, and opinions of others. Despite the intense emotions and need for independence they are feeling, twelve-year-olds should be reminded that other people's feelings matter too. Explain why respect matters in life, and insist they continue to follow family rules, participate in chores, and share family experiences—regardless of whether they feel like it in the moment or not.

3. **Self-Expression.** *Express your unique personality, and encourage those around you to also be themselves.* Twelve-year-olds have more defined personalities, styles, and interests than they did before. This is your opportunity to nurture your children's individuality and help them form opinions about who they want to be. While it is important to encourage self-expression, remind them that you still expect them to follow the rules and demonstrate the values you have taught them.

4. **Bullying.** *Do not bully or make fun of people who are different from you and your friends.* Twelve-year-olds can often be cruel without realizing how hurtful they truly are. Parents need to talk to their pre-teen about understanding and accepting the differences they may encounter among their peers.

5. **Confidence.** *Speak up, be assertive, and demonstrate confidence in yourself and your ideas.* Twelve-year-old children need to hear that they can and should have confidence in their ideas. Those who seem confident or even arrogant may actually be struggling with self-esteem issues. They need to be complimented, supported, and endorsed.

6. **Smoking.** *Smoking is a dangerous thing to try because of addiction and long-term effects.* Most smokers try their first cigarette between ages twelve and seventeen. While you may have talked to your child previously about the negative effects of smoking, now is the time to talk to them about the dangers of even trying a cigarette. Talk to your child about peer pressure, and explain that they have freedom to say no to trying things like cigarettes.

7. **Unsupervised Social Media Rules.** *Social media is a great way to stay in touch with friends and share information but you need to be extra careful with your online behavior.* Children increasingly use social media as their main form of communication. The platforms will change and evolve so there is little benefit in going into the specifics. All the Rules for using social media when supervised still apply and must be followed.

The Recommended Rules and Conversations for Thirteen-Year-Olds

What should children be learning about at age 13?

YOUR RULES AND CONVERSATION TOPICS
What else do you want to talk about?

_____

_____

_____

_____

PROGRESS REPORT
What's happened since last year?

_____

_____

_____

_____

Parent's Guide to Age 13

What's Going On?

At age thirteen, most teens feel in limbo. Their hormones are starting to rage and change the way they view themselves, other people and the world around them. Many are beginning to experiment with romantic and physical relationships. They are capable of thinking and acting more like adults, but they have to learn how to think and act appropriately for their age. Parents should be prepared to have some adult-level conversations with their thirteen-year-old in order to foster healthy relationships moving forward.

Suggested Rules and Conversations

1. **Peer Pressure.** *If your friends are pressuring you to do something you know is wrong, just say "no."* Young teens have probably experienced peer pressure from an early age, but thirteen-year-olds often become more susceptible to it. Peer pressure can be positive or negative. Positive peer pressure might include sports teams, clubs, youth groups, and other volunteer groups. Negative peer pressure influences include gangs, abusive friends, or friends without strong morals. The good news: Negative peer pressure is not as appealing to thirteen-year-olds who have strong support systems at home. To maintain influence in your teenagers' lives, develop close, open, and honest relationships with them. This does not mean they always get their way but rather that they feel comfortable coming to you if they are in trouble or having problems. Talk to your children about morals and values and why making good decisions will benefit them more in the long run than impressing their friends.

2. **Media Influence.** *Do not judge yourself by what you see on magazine covers, the internet, and TV.* Know that you are beautiful just the way you are. Television shows, social media, and other forms of

entertainment often send unhealthy messages to teens. This can result in a negative body image, inappropriate behavior, misguided values, poor social skills, and other lasting effects. Talk to your children about what they see in the media and why they shouldn't try to emulate everything they see.

Do not try to emulate celebrity behaviors that go against the morals and values you've been taught. Thirteen-year-olds need guidance to make behavioral decisions on their own, rather than basing those decisions off of what they see in celebrities' lives. There are many messages directed to your teen from television, the Internet, and social media. Parents need to make sure that their voice is also part of those messages.

3. **Cyberbullying.** *Never post hateful or hurtful comments about other people online.* The digital world has created a new and more powerful arena for bullying. Now when children are bullied, it's not just a few peers who witness their embarrassment. Instead, hateful and damaging words get posted online for everyone to see. Nearly half of kids have been bullied online, and one in four has experienced this more than once. Talk to your teens about cyberbullying—what it is, what to do if it happens to them or someone they know, and why they should never participate in this type of behavior.

4. **Dating.** *Dating should be fun and should never make you feel pressured or unsafe.* Kids start dwelling on dating more as they move into their teen years. Parents play a very important role in helping their teens learn what is healthy in a relationship and what is not. Before your teens start dating, talk to them about appropriate behavior and the consequences of experimenting with sexual acts at such a young age. Help them better understand the feelings they experience and how to manage them.

5. **Privacy.** *Do not abuse your right to privacy or you will lose it.* Thirteen-year-olds need their own personal time and space. They are on the road to becoming independent young adults, and that can change family dynamics. While privacy should be honored, make sure your teens know you still want to be part of their lives.

Explain that you will respect their privacy—unless you have reason to believe they are in danger—but that you still expect them to follow the rules you have set forth for the household.

6. **Family Time.** *Spending time with your family is still a priority, even as you become more independent.* Teens are developing friendships that are exciting and fun to them, and may start to pull away from the family. Make sure your teens know you still want to be part of their lives and that family time is still important. Find ways to engage with your teen's interests during family events to make them even more excited to embrace family relationships.

7. **Bank Account Rules.** *Create a plan for saving and managing your money.* At age thirteen, teens can co-sign with parents and open checking and savings accounts. This is a great age to start teaching children about managing money. They can practice saving and taking responsibility for their own money, but you still have access and can guide them as they learn to use these accounts. Talk to them about the difference between savings and checking accounts, how to make payments, and how to approach saving.

8. **Curfew Rules.** *Curfews are built to provide accountability and structure.* At age thirteen, teens are starting to do more with friends in the evenings and may be doing more in the evenings away from mom and dad. This new independence can be a fun thing for a teen, but they need to understand what the rules are with curfew. Talk to them about the legal curfews, as well as any personal curfew rules that you enforce. Make sure your teen understands why there are curfew rules in place to help give your child a healthy perspective toward these rules.

The Recommended Rules and Conversations for Fourteen-Year-Olds

AGE
14

What should children be learning about at age 14?

YOUR RULES AND CONVERSATION TOPICS
What else do you want to talk about?

_____

_____

_____

_____

PROGRESS REPORT
What's happened since last year?

_____

_____

_____

_____

1. Checking-In Rules
2. Safe Sex
3. Reputation
4. Unsupervised Mobile Device Rules
5. Friendship
6. Dating Rules
7. Balanced Diet
8. Alcohol

Parent's Guide to Age 14

What's Going On?

Age fourteen can be a tough, in-between stage for young teens. Some fourteen-year-olds are looking forward to driving and dating soon, while others are still hanging onto childish antics. In general, most of them are dealing with a number of complex issues related to puberty and sex, self-esteem, and growing independence.

Suggested Rules and Conversations

1. **Checking-In Rules.** *Always check in with parents about the four Ws: who, what, when, and where.* As young teens grow more independent, many start thinking they don't have to report to parents on their whereabouts. While there is a fine line between nagging and knowing, parents need to know where fourteen-year-olds are going, with whom, at what time, and what they are doing. Knowing these things can be as simple as asking them about their day, meeting their friends, and getting into their worlds a little.

2. **Safe Sex.** *If you have questions about sex, talk to parents, teachers, or other trusted adults.* Don't take your friends' word for it. By age fourteen, many teens are thinking about sex, but feel awkward talking about it or asking about it. Parents should open up that dialogue to let their child know who to talk to about questions and their feelings.

   Many young teens are also experimenting, questioning, and forming opinions about their own sexual orientation. While fourteen-year-olds might not be able or ready to discuss their own feelings, they need to have an open dialogue with adults they trust. Talk to your young teens about the different sexual orientations, how to discuss sexual orientation with friends and peers, and how to respect people regardless of their sexual orientation.

Understand that having sex too early can have serious repercussions— mentally, physically, and emotionally. Talk to parents before you engage in any physical activity. Talk to your child early and often about sex. Most children already know about sex before age fourteen, and one in ten have already had sex before age fifteen. However, by continuing the conversation, you can help to ensure your child has accurate information. Otherwise, they will learn from friends and the media. Discuss oral sex, contraceptives, STDs, pregnancy, and emotions related to being sexually active.

3. **Reputation.** *Consider how actions— online and in the real world—will affect your reputation.* Fourteen-year-olds often need reminders that what they do online affects their reputation. The world they are surrounded by encourages them to not pay attention to or care about their reputation, and therefore, parents continually need to be reminding

their teen to care and to think about their online actions.

4. **Unsupervised Mobile Device Rules.** *You are now old enough to have your own digital privacy and to be trusted to act responsibly.* All rules of using social media, email, and the Internet can now be managed directly by your child. They should never post anything on social media that they would be ashamed for adults, teachers, or future employers to see. Fourteen-year-olds are often involved in drama, gossip, and bullying. Discussing the importance of one's reputation and self-esteem helps them develop into healthy teens and better friends. Talk to your teens about the repercussions of having a bad reputation and how destructive gossip can be to other people's self-esteem. This is particularly important in the digital age, when teens must also consider the lasting nature of their online reputations. Studies indicate that half of teens are not concerned

about online behavior negatively affecting their futures. They do not realize employers might someday find pictures or questionable posts or that by releasing certain information on social media, they are allowing themselves to be targets for abuse.

5. **Friendship.** *Choose friends who treat you well, and be a good friend to them.* As kids move into their teen years, friendships become central to personal enjoyment and social interaction. Family is still important, but strong friendships help teens sort through emotions and life changes. Many of these friendships will continue into their twenties or even later into adulthood. Talk to fourteen-year-olds about the relationships they are forming. Discuss how to be a loving, supportive friend and how they can choose friends who treat them well.

6. **Dating Rules.** *Ask for permission before dating, and follow all established rules and curfews.* Fourteen is a good age for teens to start thinking about dating, but that doesn't mean they're ready for it. Studies have consistently found that teens who start dating too young are more likely to have behavioral problems than those who wait. Children who start dating at age eleven are twice as likely to have unsafe sex, use alcohol, and indulge in risky behaviors. Talk to your teens about safe dating from a physical, emotional, and mental perspective. Before you allow them to go on dates, communicate clear rules and expectations for their behavior.

Romance is new for many young teens, and they are likely to mistake romantic feelings or lust for love. Talk to your teens about what love is and what it is not. Discuss the level of seriousness in their relationships, and help them determine when they are ready to say "I love you" to someone.

7. **Balanced Diet.** *With more independence comes greater opportunity to make responsible choices—including what you eat.* While you have been more than likely educating your kids on a balanced diet all along, at age fourteen your child is going to begin making more of their own food choices since they will be eating more meals outside of the home and not within your control. For this reason it's smart to have a discussion about the benefits of a balanced diet for health and growth.

8. **Alcohol.** *Not only is it illegal for you to drink underage, the effects of consuming too much alcohol can be massively damaging.* It is likely by fourteen that children will begin experimenting with alcohol. This is a good time for a candid conversation about drinking and its effects. Explain responsible behavior and the consequences of consuming alcohol, especially as a minor. Prohibition is going to become increasingly unlikely, so explain the pros and cons instead.

The Recommended Rules and Conversations for Fifteen-Year-Olds

What should children be learning about at age 15?

YOUR RULES AND CONVERSATION TOPICS
What else do you want to talk about?

_____

_____

_____

_____

PROGRESS REPORT
What's happened since last year?

_____

_____

_____

_____

Parent's Guide to Age 15

What's Going On?

At age fifteen, most teens are pushing the limits to try new things—both good and bad. Some of their friends are probably doing things they're not allowed to do yet, and they might be tempted to grow up too fast, rather than enjoying what's left of childhood. Fifteen-year-olds are still dealing with a number of hormonal changes and physical growth, which can lead to emotional outbursts and rebellious attitudes. Parents should be prepared to help manage the emotional, physical, and mental needs of their growing fifteen-year-olds.

Suggested Rules and Conversations

1. **Household.** *Follow all household rules, and ask for permission before taking new liberties.* Fifteen-year-olds constantly ask parents for more liberties. They see other teens driving, getting jobs, dating, and enjoying freedoms they might not yet have. Because they are more assertive at this age, they are more likely to try new things without asking for permission. Rebellious activities and attitudes are not uncommon for fifteen-year-olds, so it's important to explain why certain rules and limitations are in place. By opening this dialogue, you help teens understand the limits and feel empowered in their current stage of life.

2. **Respect for Elders.** *Speak to parents and other adults with respect.* At this age, teens often feel the need to push family away. They might not rely on you as much because they are testing out their independence. As long as they are taking care of their responsibilities and following your rules, encourage them to keep developing their independence. Remind them about the importance of family, but don't take it personally if they

would rather spend more time with friends than with you. At the same time, remind your teen that the same manners they learned as a child still apply.

3. **Drugs and Alcohol.** *Indulging in drugs and alcohol is more risky than you realize.* By age fifteen, the part of a teenager's brain which supports craving (i.e., the amygdala) is developed, but the prefrontal cortical areas that support the capacity to regulate behavior keeps maturing until about age twenty-five. This means teenagers are more likely to take unsafe risks, such as abusing drugs or alcohol. Educate your teen about the effects of different substances. Consider sharing your own experiences to help teens think wisely about drug abuse. Often bringing yourself to their level can help them learn from your past mistakes or understand the gravity of addiction in people they know personally.

4. **Abuse.** *Never put up with mental, physical, or sexual abuse in romantic relationships.* Stand up for yourself, and seek help from trusted adults. Fifteen-year-olds might feel pressure to be in relationships that are emotionally, sexually, or mentally abusive. This is not only dangerous for teens, but it can also lead to unhealthy views about romantic love that continue into adulthood. Talk to your teens about these issues— including why it's important to speak up for themselves when they are feeling uncomfortable and how to seek help. Get to know your children's significant others, and watch for warning signs of abuse.

5. **Depression and Suicide.** *Talk to parents or other trusted adults if you have suicidal thoughts or if your friends discuss harming themselves.* Many adolescents suffer from a depressive disorder by age eighteen. Boys and girls experience depression at the same rate, however girls are

more likely to have outward symptoms. Left untreated, depression can lead to suicidal thoughts or actions or other forms of self-harm. Talk to your teens about depression, and watch them closely for warning signs. Teens often share their intimate feelings with other teens, rather than adults. Even if your teens are not depressed or suicidal, they might have friends struggling with these issues who confide in them. Fifteen-year-olds need to know when to keep a friend's confidence and when to seek the help of an adult or mental health professional. Talk your teens through different 'what-if' scenarios. Help them understand that depression is a serious but treatable condition, and that some actions can't be undone.

6. **Conflict Resolution.** *Learn how to talk about and resolve conflicts with family and friends.* Fifteen-year-olds often have conflicts with friends and family. Many of these spats may seem small and easily resolvable, so use these occurrences as an opportunity to coach your teen on the conflict resolution skills they'll need throughout their lives. Talk to them about how to be respectful, understanding, and assertive when discussing issues and mending relationships.

7. **Credit Card Rules.** *Only consider opening a credit card if you are prepared to follow the boundaries and rules established when using it.* Teens may start pressing for their own credit cards. For those who have jobs and are starting to drive, this might not be a bad idea. If you have a good credit score, getting a card in your teens' names can help them start building credit. Just keep a tight rein on how the card is used, and monitor transactions diligently. Talk to your teens about boundaries and rules for using credit cards, how credit works, and the consequences of racking up too much debt.

8. **Body Image.** *If you're worried about your weight, talk to parents or your doctor before beginning any new diets.* Most fifteen-year-olds—both girls and boys—are dealing with body-image issues, which often lead to serious body-image disturbance and eating disorders. If your teens are under- or overweight, talk to them about how this makes them feel and suggest healthy alternatives to the fad diets that many adults and children buy into. Talk to them about the importance of exercise and physical activity, and look for ways the whole family can be active together. During this impressionable age, avoid calling yourself "fat" or complaining about your own body. Children often learn to love or hate their bodies based on the dialogues they've been hearing from parents.

Do not take weight-loss supplements without a doctor's approval. Some teens will think they can make sound decisions about medicine, including weight-loss supplements. Talk to your teen, and make sure they understand what supplements and medications should be discussed with a doctor before taking. Parents need to learn to listen to their teen to understand why they want to use a particular supplement in the first place. There is usually an underlying reason, and parents should be talking with their teen to be able to understand their teen's motivation for using supplements.

9. **Part-time Job Rules.** *If you desire you may now engage in a part-time job as long you can balance school, family, extracurricular activities, a social life, and work.* Most fifteen-year-olds are capable of working part-time if their other commitments allow. Teenagers will want the independence of having their own income and the responsibility of handling a real job. The experience they gain from a boss and the demands of work will be invaluable. Make sure you have an active dialogue about the challenges of work and the behavior necessary to be successful.

The Recommended Rules and Conversations for Sixteen-Year-Olds

What should children be learning about at age 16?

YOUR RULES AND CONVERSATION TOPICS
What else do you want to talk about?

_____

_____

_____

_____

PROGRESS REPORT
What's happened since last year?

_____

_____

_____

_____

1. Career
2. College
3. Family Time
4. Sleep
5. Stress
6. Saving and Investing Rules
7. Politics Rules
8. Drug Abuse
9. Community Service Rules

Parent's Guide to Age 16

What's Going On?

Most sixteen-year-olds have many things going on; they are juggling school, part-time jobs, and extracurricular activities. They might also be navigating new friendships and romantic relationships. Teens at this age are beginning to think about life after high school, which can be both exciting and stressful. They will need guidance from parents and teachers for making adult decisions.

Suggested Rules and Conversations

1. **Career.** *Start thinking about what careers interest you and which colleges you might want to attend.* Many sixteen-year-olds are thinking about what they want to do after high school—go to college or trade school, join the military, or get jobs. They might also be considering career options, as that dictates the path they will take after high school. While still teens, sixteen-year-olds are forced to start thinking about

adulthood and major life choices. Talk to your children about their long-term interests. Be careful not to push your own agenda or desires but rather to help them think through the options that appeal to them.

2. **College.** *Talk to your guidance counselor about what you need to be doing now, to prepare for applying to college.* Parents should encourage their teen to talk to other trusted individuals, like a guidance counselor, for insight and advice about the future. Many colleges require applicants to have extracurricular and leadership experience. Make sure you understand your child's goals and a path to get there.

3. **Family Time.** *Spend some time at home, bonding with parents and family.* As teens mature and form deeper opinions and beliefs, you can engage on a deeper level with them. Many foundations for lifelong adult friendships happen in these middle

The Birthday Rules: Critical Conversations to Have with Your Children

teen years, and relationships with parents are no exception. In fact, three quarters of teenagers enjoy spending time with Mom, and about the same amount like hanging out with Dad. This is a great time to get to know your teens and to truly listen to their opinions and beliefs.

4. **Sleep.** *Make time to get enough sleep.* Many sixteen-year-olds think sleep is overrated. They worry they might miss out on something by sleeping. They think they need the time to talk to friends on the phone and be more social on the Internet. Talk to your teens about why sleep is important—for their health, mood, and concentration at school. One thing to keep in mind: Teenagers may have different circadian rhythms than adults, so their bodies might not be ready for sleep at "bedtime." They also tend to spend a lot of time napping during the day.

5. **Stress.** *Talk to trusted adults if you're feeling stressed, overwhelmed, or anxious.* Most teens are under more stress than adults often realize. Between school, sports, friendships, jobs, and family dynamics, teens deal with a lot of pressure. Talk to your teen about coping skills and how to handle different types of stress, and model healthy stress-busting behaviors for your teens. These skills will help them for the rest of their lives.

6. **Saving and Investing Rules.** *Start saving or investing extra money as soon as you can.* Parents can start investing for their children at any age, but as teens start thinking about adulthood and their first "real" jobs, it's a good time to teach them about the importance of investing for the future and how to do so. At age sixteen, children are still living with parents and are willing to listen to their advice about money. During and after college, parents' advice might not be as heeded. If you don't know much about investing, take your teen to visit a broker and learn together.

7. **Politics Rules.** *Read the news and start to be aware of what's going on in the nation.* At sixteen, your child is still a few years away from voting, but this can be a crucial time to guide your teen in thinking about national and world issues. Encourage your teen to form political opinions and to justify those beliefs with solid reasons. Let your home be a safe place for your teen to talk about political issues, whether or not they align with your personal beliefs.

8. **Drug Abuse.** *If you or someone you know is using illegal substances, reach out to a parent or teacher.* By age sixteen, many teens have experimented with drugs and/or alcohol. Some teens may already have serious addiction problems due to use of these substances. Keep the conversation open with your teen about the effects of drugs and alcohol. Talk regularly with them, and make sure they know where to turn if they or someone they know needs help.

9. **Community Service Rules.** *Volunteering builds character and empathy—and a great way to build social skills.* If your child has not already experienced community service through a youth group, religious organization, or another avenue, this is a good time to discuss how they can become involved. Volunteering time is not only a good way to teach appreciation for what kids have been given, it's also a great way to build social skills. This is also a good age to discuss the sacrifices made by those who serve their community and country.

The Birthday Rules Conclusion

By gathering all the data we could find from developmental experts the world over, we hope we have created a tool that made your impossibly difficult task as a parent a tiny bit easier!

However, as information proliferates children will continue to be exposed to topics earlier, technology will continue to advance, and the experts will come up with ever-new research (only to have another study refute that one). The goal of the *Birthday Rules* is to create a fun, flexible framework, nothing more.

Change the rules for whatever works best for you and your family. Change the rules for any new technologies which are developed, such as when a child can handle virtual reality. Change the rules as the experts change their opinions. But create the space in a structured format to have conversations, and grant permission. The consistency of the process, the review, the conversation, and the consequences are the only tools we hope to offer.

References by Age

Age 6

http://www.themotherco.com/2013/01
/teaching-manners-to-kids/

http://childparenting.about.com/od
/physicalemotionalgrowth/a/6-Year-Old
-Child-Emotional-Development.htm

http://www.webmd.com/parenting/features
/chores-for-children

https://www.commonsensemedia.org/blog
/5-ways-to-talk-to-your-kids-about
-swearing-and-why

Age 7

http://www.cdc.gov/ncbddd/childdevelopment
/positiveparenting/middle.html

http://www.greatschools.org/special-education
/health/731-developmental-milestones
-your-7-year-old-child.gs

http://childparenting.about.com/od
/physicalemotionalgrowth/tp
/Child-Development-Your-Seven-Year
-Old-Child.htm

Age 8

http://www.cnn.com/2011/TECH/gaming
.gadgets/06/29/video.games.kids.wired/

http://www.theguardian.com/technology
/2014/jun/02/parents-guide-video-games
-playstation-xbox-wii-apps-children

http://www.pbs.org/parents
/childdevelopmenttracker/eight/

http://www.kidsgrowth.com/resources
/articledetail.cfm?id=1136

http://www.networkworld.com/
article/2225579/microsoft-subnet
/most-parents-allow-unsupervised-
internet-access-to-children-at-age-8.html

http://betanews.com/2013/10/15/at-what
-age-should-children-be-allowed-to-use
-the-internet/

Age 9

http://www.babycenter.com/0_how-to-talk
-to-your-child-about-sex_67908.bc

http://lifestyle.howstuffworks.com/family
/parenting/tweens-teens/10-tips-for
-parenting-preteens.htm

http://lifestyle.howstuffworks.com/family
/parenting/tweens-teens/10-tips-for
-parenting-preteens.htm#page=2

http://lifestyle.howstuffworks.com/family
/parenting/tweens-teens/10-tips-for
-parenting-preteens.htm#page=5

http://www.webmd.boots.com/children
/guide/childhood-milestones-age-9
?page=3

Age 10

http://childparenting.about.com/od/socialdevelopment/a/10-Year-Olds-And-Social-Development.htm

http://childparenting.about.com/od/physicalemotionalgrowth/tp/Child-Development-Your-Ten-Year-Old-Child.htm

http://lifestyle.howstuffworks.com/family/parenting/tweens-teens/10-tips-for-parenting-preteens.htm#page=4

http://www.dailymail.co.uk/news/article-2552658/More-half-children-use-social-media-age-10-Facebook-popular-site-youngsters-join.html

http://childparenting.about.com/od/physicalemotionalgrowth/tp/Child-Development-Your-Ten-Year-Old-Child.htm

Age 11

http://www.cyh.com/HealthTopics/HealthTopicDetails.aspx?p=114&np=122&id=1865

http://raisingchildren.net.au/articles/preteens_development_nutshell.html

Age 12

http://www.cyh.com/HealthTopics/HealthTopicDetails.aspx?p=114&np=122&id=1865

http://raisingchildren.net.au/articles/preteens_development_nutshell.html

http://www.huffingtonpost.com/galit-breen/14-essential-truths-about-raising-a-tween-girl_b_6136266.html

Age 13

http://www.a-better-child.org/page/923604

http://everydaylife.globalpost.com/medias-positive-negative-influence-teenagers-10506.html

https://www.dosomething.org/facts/11-facts-about-cyber-bullying

http://msue.anr.msu.edu/news/signs_of_a_healthy_teenage_dating_relationship

http://parentingteens.about.com/od/agesandstages/a/Emotional-Development-Your-13-Year-Old-Teen.htm

http://www.ourkidsandmoney.com/should-i-get-my-child-a-checking-account/

Age 14

http://www.drphil.com/articles/article/51

http://www.familycircle.com/teen/parenting/sex-talk/talking-to-teens-about-sex/?page=2

http://teen.allwomenstalk.com/ways-to-avoid-getting-a-bad-reputation

http://www.teenhealthfx.com/answers/relationships/46824

http://www.essentialkids.com.au/older-kids
/behaviour-and-discipline-for-older-kids
/when-should-children-be-allowed-to
-date-20140616-3a6ah.html

Age 15

http://parentingteens.about.com/od
/agesandstages/a/Emotional
-Development-Your-15-Year-Old-
Teen.htm
http://www.healthychildren.org/English
/ages-stages/teen/substance-abuse
/Pages/Talk-to-Your-Teen-About-Drugs
-And-Keep-Talking.aspx
http://parentingteens.about.com/od
/teensexuality/fl/When-is-Your-Teen
-Ready-for-a-Relationship.htm
http://www.cyh.com/HealthTopics/
HealthTopicDetails.aspx?p=243&np
=291&id=2183
http://www.creditcards.com/credit-card-news
/price-mueller-piggybacking-kids-to-good
-credit-scores-1377.php
http://www.ncbi.nlm.nih.gov/pubmed
/16219362

Age 16

http://parentingteens.about.com/od
/talktoyourteen/ht/teen_future.htm
http://www.livescience.com/13850-10-facts
-parent-teen-brain.html
http://parentingteens.about.com/
od/16yearoldteens/a/Behavior-And-Daily
-Routines-Your-16-Year-Old-Teen.htm
http://www.getrichslowly.org/guide-to
-money/invest/when-should-i-start
-investing.html

About the Authors

Jeffrey Wald is a serial entrepreneur having directly raised three companies, and, as an investor and adviser, helped raised about one hundred more. Jeff is the proud uncle to three nephews and three nieces. In addition, Jeff is a renowned speaker on startups and growing companies. He has a BS and MS from Cornell University and an MBA from Harvard.

Rachel Marsh, Ph.D. is an Associate Professor of Medical Psychology in the Division of Child Psychiatry at Columbia University Medical Center. She is the mother of three: Milo, Lyla, and Ruby. Dr. Marsh speaks worldwide and has published papers on brain function and development in health and illnesses such as eating and anxiety disorders.

Thank You from the Authors

So many people were helpful in bringing this project to life. We would like to thank the great team at Post Hill Press, the talented literary agent Becky Sweren, Caitlin McCormick for her editing, the Work Market team for their support, and Karen Leland for all her research and writing. A huge thank you to Mike and Julie and the parenting example they set with Jonah, Eli, and Evi. Last, we could not have written this book without the support of our families, most importantly our Moms and Dads. So, to Phyllis and Bill Wald, and to Lisa and Fred Marsh, as well as Adam, Milo, Iyla, and Ruby—thank you!

Notes

Notes

Notes